Every Day
with

A Himalayan Master

365 Sacred Gems
of
Inspiration and Wisdom

Yogiraj Gurunath Siddhanath

2022

Every Day with a Himalayan Master
By Yogiraj Gurunath Siddhanath

First Edition Published in July 2022

Alight Publications
PO Box 277, Live Oak,
CA 95953

ISBN 978-1-931833-60-8

Printed in the United States of America

Open the petals of your heart and
let the light and love pour through!
Honey drop and dew, honey drop and dew
This nectar of Life permeates me and you!

HAPPY NEW YEAR!

Let not precious moments slip by
SEEK NOW! the ultimate truth
Jivahamsa spread your wings to fly
Immortal realms which death defy

-YOGIRAJ SATGURUNATH SIDDHANATH

2

Yoga is the absorption of Soul into Spirit, whereby
Sorrow and desire creating karma dissolve, consequently,
Freeing one's soul bound to the cycle of birth and death
giving it
The final liberation – Niranjana Nirvana

The undifferentiated consciousness of
the master
gravitates itself into the light-mind existence
of the thought-mind of the seeker,
thus transforming the seeker's mind
to his own consciousness;
to the degree of the attunement of
that mind with
the Master's consciousness.

Let the Fresh Breeze of the New Year take the form of Pran and move up and down your spine...

As I whirl when sprayed
with the seven colors of Holi
I become colorless and free
from all pride and prejudice.

6

I am the Sun you are my ray,
You must become the whole.
By good conduct and service.
Your character shall mould.
By devotional meditation,
I - your spirit shall unfold.
The ray becoming the blazing Sun,
Yourself as me behold !

7

The Non-Being Essentiality
He goes beyond the naked singularity,
His mass is infinite.
He experiences his center everywhere
and his circumference nowhere.

8

The more you trust
in God, the more
trustable He becomes

While experiencing the various stages
of spiritual awareness,
one has to be true to oneself.
Remember that the great sages...
alive through the ages,
can see through the hearts and
minds of humanity.
They know exactly where each individual
stands in the hierarchy
of his personal evolution and the depth
of his devotion to God.

10

Birth and death are a chapter in your life story,
but you as the immortal river of Livingness,
Flow on!

Experiences are benchmarks to spur the individual soul in its evolutionary path.

All those who meditate with single-minded purpose shall be blessed by their guiding Masters. They will get inspirational experiences according to their evolutionary needs.

12

There is no temple greater than
the human body,
there is no prayer greater than the breath, and
there is no God greater than the Self

We are all nothingness playing
with the frivolous thoughts of
our imagination as
the Silent Watcher looks on,

The ultimate healing is realizing God,
the ultimate magic is knowing God,
the ultimate yoga is becoming God

15

Suddenly, there was an inconceivable flash that came from the aurora borealis of Babaji's light. It was the mother of all lights. So His Lightness Light which lights that light which lights the light of all our souls was this indescribable light - a great Nothingness of such truth that it was immaterial. As the light actualized into 'Non-being Essentiality' - the essence of nothing, Its Majesty ignited all existence. The whole of nature and creation stood in awe with folded hands and bowed head.

God does not exist. Existence gods
and is godding all the time to
reaffirm its own existence.
God can be without existence but
existence can not be without God

That which exists after everything ceases is
the everlasting Reality which
people call by many names yet is called
The Nameless One

18

Man lives in a bedlam of misery
created by his own thoughts.

If we go deep into the meaning of
Guru: Gu is derived from Guhya which
means "hidden knowledge of spiritual gravity"
and Ru means "light of knowingness"
so the Satguru is "he who brings to light
the gravity of God inherent to Man"

Pleasures nor palaces exude
the bliss of solitude.
Attunement with the self alone
gives that final beatitude

I drink oh drink thee Sun of life,
your roaring radiance rinse me through,
gushing through spine with sizzling joy,
I thy Divinity enjoy

Watch the eye
For life is fleeing
Don't let the day go by
Practice diligently
For the answer…
Lies Within

Where supremist love doth reign,
Sat Chit Ananda by name,
who ever was even is now,
will ever be the same

Just as no two snowflakes have the same shape
but all are the same snow,
so also humans with different mindsets are
sourced in the same Soul Spirit

The sun of enlightenment shines
eternally in every human heart.
Yogiraj Satgurunath Siddhanath

Breath links the human body to
divine consciousness.
It is a bridge between humanity and divinity

Live your life like the Sun –
incinerate yourself to
explode light and life to humanity

Gruhastha (householder) yoga is a challenge
whose ordeals are far tougher than
sanyastha (renunciate) yoga

The upward and downward motion in the spine generates tremendous Love and the spine is spiritually magnetized.

The yogi becomes the process of Yoga.

The yogi becomes the Yoga.

The pilgrim, the path, and the goal become One.

Kriya Yoga chisels you into
the God that you are

Tamed and tuned to natures flow,
mind melts into the open glow,
which radiates from the soul within
where wisdoms mystic fire is king.
In joy and sorrow, light and dark,
you ever that eternal spark.
In honor and dishonor too,
you constant yogi ever new

समाधि सिद्धि:ईश्वरप्रणिधानात ॥

Iswhwar Pranidhan

From the devotional offerings of your negative ego and mind to the Lord and SatGuru you are absorbed in His grace. By heartful *bhakti* and by offering your ego in the fire of that devotion is the ego dissolved

The Guru is
the space between
duality and
divinity

34

I am there for you as
the Presence,
you will walk alone no more

Oh! Supreme Guru of the nature of bliss,
Sanctify and make my heart full of joy.
Thou art knowledge personified,
full of Spirit and essence of truth,
make me unto Thy likeness Thou King of Yogis
who dispels negativity and disease,
embodiment of Enlightenment and Peace.
To such a Divine Guru, my ceaseless salutations.

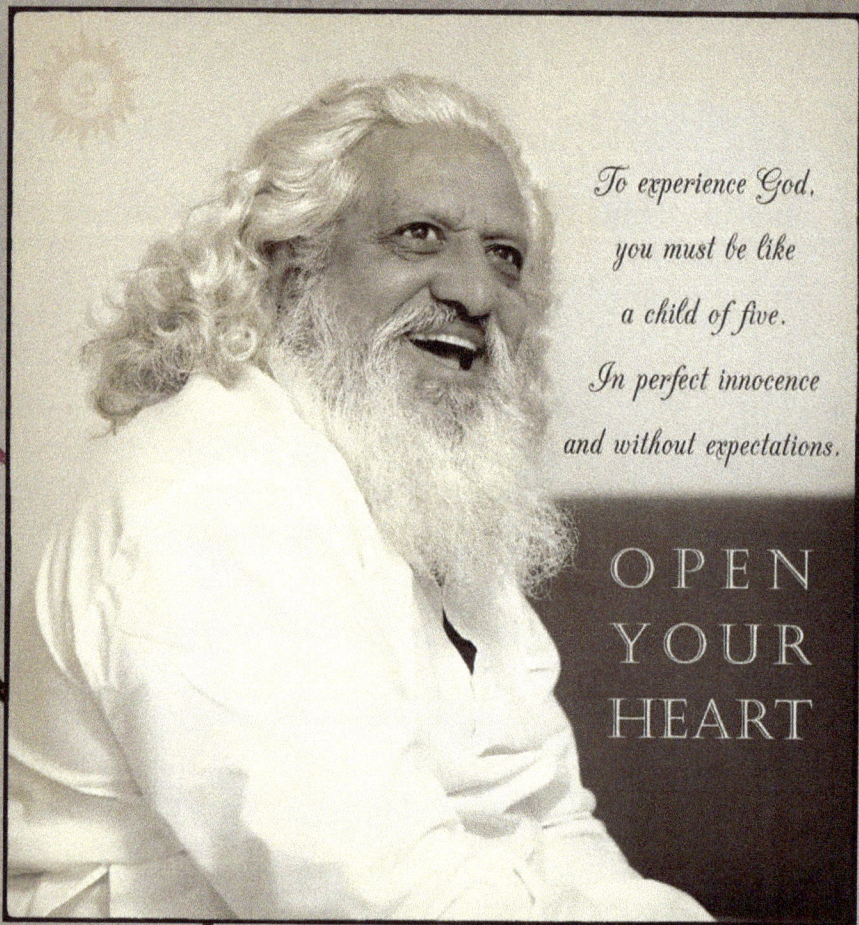

To experience God,
you must be like
a child of five.
In perfect innocence
and without expectations.

OPEN YOUR HEART

When you are aware of your body
you are a body
When you are aware of your mind
you are mind
When you are aware of your soul
you are enlightened!

Fame nor position matter to
one's inner life of peace.
Virtues used as virtues sake
cause all sorrow to cease

Achieve

Earth Peace through Self-Peace

By Realizing

Humanity, Our Uniting Religion, Breath, Our Uniting Prayer, Consciousness, Our Uniting God

Yogiraj Siddhanath

To repay what you have sown is
God's mathematical law.
All wrongs must be redressed indeed.
This fact it has no flaw.

Yoga is the practice of the union of
the individual soul (Jiva) with
the Supreme Spirit (Shiva)

The mind wanders and wonders and
wonders why it wanders because
it is the nature of the mind
to wander

The divine masters or the avatars do not simply come, bestow grace, and give you samadhi. They give it to you because you loved and practiced yoga in your past lives. Put your shoulder to the wheel of Sadhana. Be assiduous and practice, be pure, go in the direction of your spiritual practice of Shiva-Shakti. Do Babaji Kriya Yoga and the fruit will be yours in this life or the next.

Meditate like your hair is on fire

Live your life like the Sun –
incinerate yourself to
explode light and life to humanity

I'm Burning In My Love
For Thee Eternal Infinite
I Cannot Rest In Peace Now
Till I Do Become Thy Light !!

-YOGIRAJ SATGURUNATH SIDDHANATH

Dancing with thine immortal light,
Each cell is suffused with joy of life.
I glorify this gift, oh Lord,
no Emperor can ever afford

To transmute the minds of sincere seekers of yoga into a higher state of consciousness is the purpose of my work.

Your soul is pure awareness
covered by sheaths of your body and mind.
It is your True Self of the same
Essence of Cosmic
Awareness Shiva

I Am There For You!

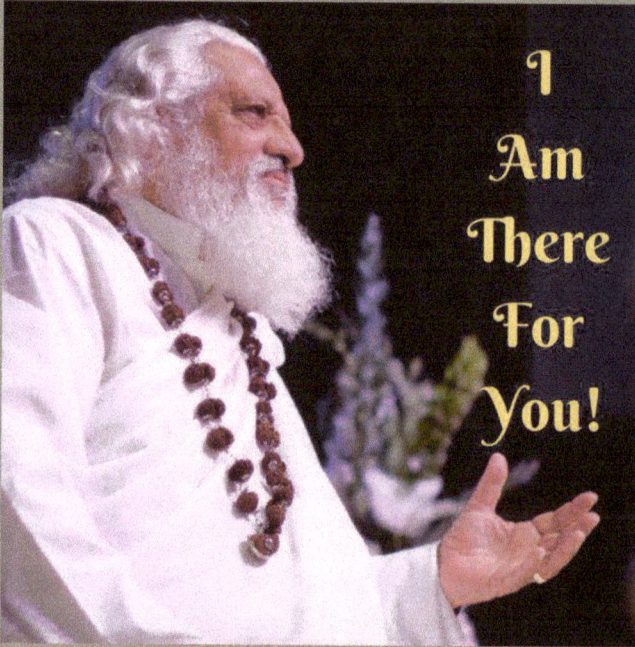

Right from the moment you sincerely do Kriya Yoga, it gives me access to work in and through you. This along with Siddhanath Surya is one of the best boosters of the immune system.

As you all have experienced me when you think of me, you may collectively chant OM at the time of your choosing. After Kriya and Surya, the loud and mental chanting of Omkar becomes potent.

A thought-free state of
Universal Awareness is
Enlightenment.
Such an avasta is moksha.

The education of yogic realization is achieved when the vacillations of the collective mind cease.

Philosophy tries to explain Life,
but never succeeds.

Philosophy promises to solve Life,
but never solves anything .
All those promises remain unfulfilled.

Kriya Yog makes no effort to explain Life.
It teaches you that Life is a quest,
not a question, a mystery,not a problem.

Kriya Yog does not teach you to be curious
about life. It teaches you to Live It.

In Philosophy the mystery remains,
                    YOU remain.
In Kriya Yog, the mystery disappears,
                    YOU disappear.

At times when
you are enmeshed in
thought waves and mental images,
then your true identity
as the Atmic Seer is lost.

The cessation of the transformations of the
mind may be achieved by:
Abhyasa - sustained practice of withdrawal of
the senses from their objects.
Vairagya - dispassion to the ways of the world
and its temptations.
Refuse to be swayed
by the emotional pendulum of
attraction and repulsion.

The sustained effort taken to
attain a
tranquil mind,
free of fluctuations,
is called
practice.

Sees the darkness within yourself
before you can talk of light
and darkness in others.

When you have overcome
every temptation and
thirst not for worldly things
then you have reached the
first stage of
mastering your desires.

For true spiritual seekers to
proceed on the path,
they must develop the
four foundations for enlightenment:
faith in your ability to practice,
heroic dedication to succeed,
constant reminder of the ultimate goal, and
the Master's guidance which evolves you.

Maha Shivratri

Celebrate the eternal aspect of Shiva
within your own consciousness.
Shiva, the Supreme Deity, resides in the
temple of all human beings.

Concentrated effort in yoga is
the way to Enlightenment, but
total surrender and personal devotion to
the Lord is also important for salvation.
The Lord is the Divine Indweller
who is outwardly expressed as
SatGuru

The true Self is
unbounded by time and space.
This being is the primeval
Master of all Masters.

Om is the light-sound explosion,
the Bang which occurred at the
beginning of Time.
A spiritual essence smaller than the
nucleus of an atom,
compressed within which was the
mind and matter of the whole Universe
exploded 13.7 billion years ago, and
its ripple effects towards Creation,
as well as Evolution are still reverberating in
the waters of Eternal Space.

"Those who know it tell it not and those who tell it know it not."

- Yogiraj Gurunath Siddhanath

Use these four virtuous attitudes
towards people in order for you to
have a tranquil mind:
Friendliness towards the happy.
Compassion towards the suffering.
Delight towards the virtuous.
Indifference towards the non-virtuous.

When the vacillations of the mind disap-
pear, it becomes as pure and transparent as a
high quality gem that reflects
the form of gemstones placed near it.
As you go deeper, your mind absorbs
itself into the object you are meditating on.
At this point,
the knower,
the knowing and the
known become
one.

Look back and get experience,
Look forward and see hope,
Look around and find reality,

Look within to
Realize
Yourself

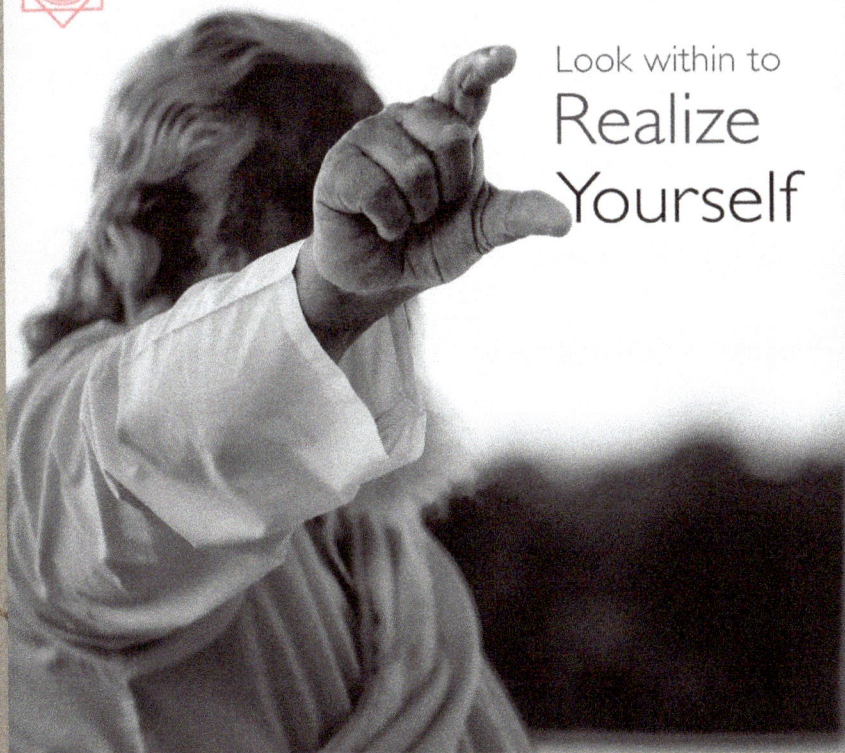

They call me Death and yet
I take them to eternity.
Oh this paradox of Ignorance
Deludes humanity.

Men steeped in earthly ignorance
Do dread me as their foe
Knowing not that to their Souls
The light of truth I show.

Rejoice then when I come to you,
Each time at end of life.
It is to take you in my arms,
From worldly storms and strife.

I myself say, you cannot come
across a more ignorant man
than me. This is the truth.
I have come from nowhere
I have not reached anywhere,

I am simply now and here.

But, if you can follow what this
ignorant man has taught you,
you will soon realise the same
truth.

God is not a Goal,
God is what is Now and Here.

Hamsa Eternal how may we
Being work-bound yet be everfree?
Enlightened action is the key
Which gives that final liberty!

Enlightened action doth arise
Within your crystal conscious skies
Experience of the Hamsa Still
Make you know Divinity's will

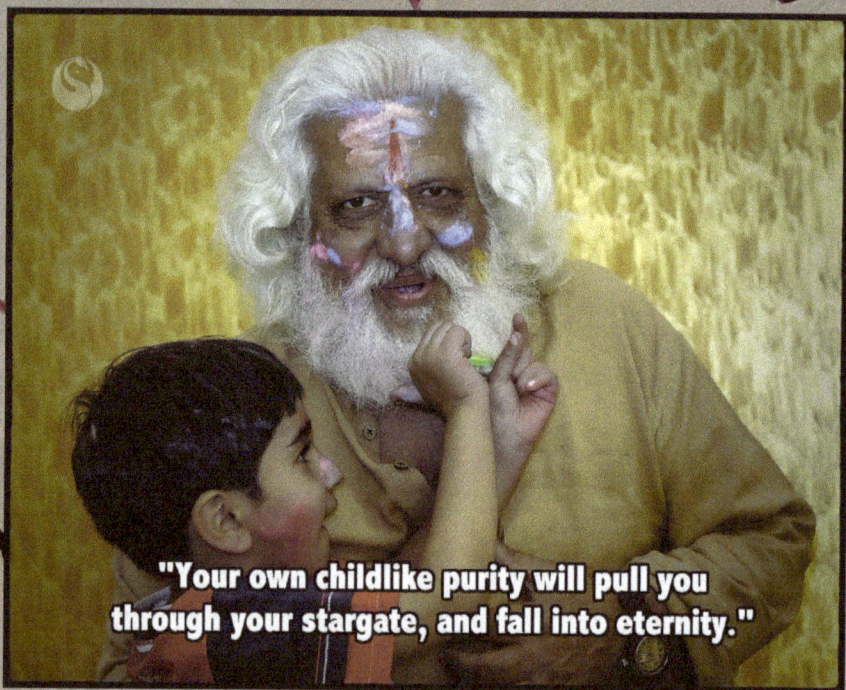

"Your own childlike purity will pull you
through your stargate, and fall into eternity."

I am a dweller of that boundless country
Where Lord Goraksha is King of all souls.
There he breathes the Ham Sah
we are being breathed
He does the work all sit at rest
Oh! Brother we all sit in tranquillity.

I brushed aside the curtain
Of the window of mine eye
And beheld the sparkling Truth,
That within me did reply.
Oh Man you're not this house of flesh
Which sleeps decays and dies.
You are immortal consciousness,
King of the earth and skies.

All wrongs must be redressed indeed,
This fact it has no flaw.
All rights are rewarded
In proportion and no more.
To each one is meted out
His exact and proper score.

You can never meet God. How can you meet him? You don't know his whereabouts, you don't know his address.

But God is going to meet you.
He is in search of you constantly, and when you are ready he will meet you.

Practice will make you ready,
Perseverance will make you perfect.

So carry these two mantras with you:
Practice and Persevere.
Let these two be the goals.
Let your whole life revolve around them, and very soon you will be empty.

Then God will pour himself into you

To the Truth is Truth begot,
The liar gets his own.
So make your actions such,
Whose reactions you don't moan.
To the likeness of your thinking,
Shall your character be made.
Dig deep your mind for noble thoughts,
With intellectual spade.

Oh Hamsa Spirit of my soul
What is my final goal?
Is there any such remedy to
Break this karmic hold?
This duality of opposites,
Teach me to override.
Take me with thee oh Spirit free,
On to the other side.

The root of meditation is the Guru's form.
The root of worship is the Guru's feet.
The root of mantra is the Guru's word.
The root of liberation is the Guru's grace.

I am the Sun you are my ray,
you must become the whole.
By good conduct and service,
Your character shall mould.
By devotional meditation,
I – your spirit shall unfold.
The ray become the blazing Sun,
Yourself as Me behold!

How strange this world of Maya is
How gripping and how strong
In this cosmic motion picture
The right appears all wrong.

The false appears as truth
And the truth appears all false
On this Dancing dream of Maya
Is a paradoxal waltz.

Today we live throbbing with life.
Tomorrow we are gone
Mere shadows in a waking dream
We leave this world forlorn.

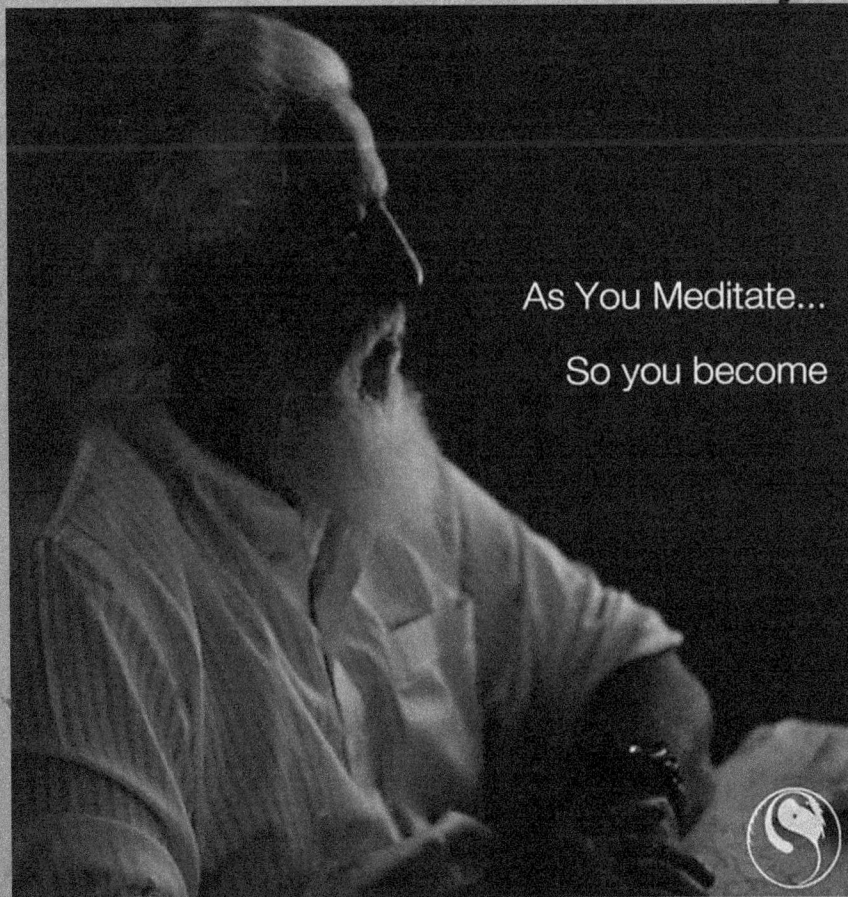

As You Meditate...

So you become

Arise Oh Children of the Lord.
Immortal souls Divine.
Break your delusive Mayic sleep,
Race for your home sublime.

As a leaking vessel never can fill
Waters of Life so pure and still
So distracted mind fails to retain
Wisdoms nectar in its brain

How do we keep from getting attached? By working out that experience and practicing Kriya Yoga.

The practice of Kriya creates detachment to the object of the senses, which prevents the progress of the soul. In the attachment you must see God, then God will take care.

To ease disease of random mind
A remedy suitable we must find
A rhythmic breathing tension free
With absorption the sovereign key

Time spent in solitude of mind
Enrichens wine of any kind
Where silence stills the finest brew
That vintage tastes like honey dew.

Shiva is the integrated consciousness
of the universe
He is our True Self
Our Divine Indweller
Our thought free state of Awareness
Any and every one can realize Him
through Kriya Yoga spinal breath

Think with your heart.
Love with your mind.

From thy elysian fountain rays
I drink immortal Pranic Life
Rejuven Body and my mind
Dissolve all worldly woe and strife!

Dancing with thine immortal light
Each cell suffused with joy of Life
I glorify this gift oh Lord
No Emperor ever can afford!

If you call me, your breath will lengthen.
I will be present with you. Just talk to me -
talk to the photo.

Orange elixirs wine sublime
Flows glows in every fiber mine
Filling me with thy Bliss sublime
Making me to My Self Divine!

Kundalini bless me with thy blaze
Delusion, suffering fear efface
Spine darkness; with they lightening light
Fragrance me ! Negative karma ignite !

This world is but a thoughtfulness of
Mayic atoms intertwined
Whose electrons are energy of
light essence sublime.

A Satguru knows the myriad pathways to Supreme Truth. An embodiment of Divine grace, he takes upon himself negative karma, thus freeing some of the obstacles lying in the path of the disciple.

He does so selflessly for the betterment of the disciple's health and spiritual progress.

100

This world our sages did perceive is
mindstuff materialized.
In relative sequence it is built
deceiving mortal eyes.

All that is composed they knew
must get decomposed
Where then does reality lie?
All matter being composed.

That all pervading consciousness of
stillness through Eternity
Must of necessity proclaim its ultimate reality.

Composed of nothing yet of which
all else is sure composed
It stands supreme beyond all dreams
eternally reposed.

no matter
where you are
...

ALWAYS
MEDITATE

Kriya Yoga is the unity with the
Divine through desireless action.
Tapa, Svadhyaya and Ishvar Pranidhan are the
means to achieving this yoga of liberation.
Tapa is discipline,
Svadhyaya is Self-study and
Ishwar Pranidhan is ego surrender and
devotion to the Divine.

The purpose of practicing Kriya Yoga is to reduce and stem the
five causes of suffering which distract the mind.
In doing so, the purified mind is habitually trained to enter its natural state of Samprajnata Samadhi.

The five primal causes of suffering are:
Avidya - ignorance of your true Self
Asmita - egoism and its self- centredness
Raga - attachment to pleasure
Dvesha - aversion to pain
Abhinivesha - clinging to life from
fear of death.

"There is no temple greater than the human body,
There is no prayer greater than the breath,
and There is no God greater than the Self."

Yogiraj Gurunath Siddhanath

Dvesha is the aversion that follows
pain which grows from the dreaded
fear that you will lose your happiness.
Do not depend on externals
for your happiness.
The answer lies within.

The mind's fluctuations of
the five sufferings are overcome
by meditation in Kriya Yoga called
Paravasta.
This is where you raise your consciousness
above the mind's lake of disturbing thoughts
and thereby sever the link between
the buddhic mind and Atmic Consciousness,
allowing the kleshas to
die their own death.

The Yogi, A Divine Superman!

"Who pursues the Divine with single-minded purpose...
Whose passion for God consumes his entire life...
A pilgrim, an ascetic,
who gives his all to seek his Beloved Lord..."

The Yogi possess nothing yet owns the world!

From the book Babaji The Lightning Standing Still by

To the wise inscerning yogi
all is misery. This comes from
the five afflictions born of the three gunas or
subatomic particles.
This pain can arise as a
direct consequence of an action
in the form of anguish from unfulfilled desires
and torment from the unwanted, or
as a samskara.
Pain can also arise as a
conflict between thoughts and
the primal natural forces of desire or gunas.

111

For the sake of
the Atmic Seer alone
does nature,
the seen creation,
exist.

Ignorance of the true Self is the
cause of the illusory union of
that Self with
the mayic and buddhic nature
of the world.

Live God, Die God
Breathe God, Eat God,
Drink God, God, God,
God God, God God,
God God

The force of past life desires impels
the Atma to identify with the intellect.
The remedy is viveka,
sustained inscerning practice of
identifying with Atmic Consciousness and
not buddhic intellect, then by
Khyatir, effulgent intuitive vision
asserting yourself to be
divine Consciousness, the Purusha.

When you are disturbed by
unwholesome and negative
thoughts and emotions try to
meditate on their opposite qualities.
These are called the
Pratipaksha Bhavana meditations.

You are God to the extent you know God!
You are Enlightened now
But you put your hands upon your eyes
And cry you cannot see.

To be the Seer
Take the hands of your mind
Off the Eyes of your Soul
And you shall see . . .
Your Divinity.

Every thought, word or deed of
violence, selfishness and lust,
directed toward yourself or others
creates negative karma.
To remedy this,
you must apply the
opposite pratipaksha qualities of
peace, generosity and a clear heart.

By being totally content with
life and graciously
accepting life's conditions as a
part of your karma,
you are thereby able to
progress smoothly on
your path of evolution.

From the devotional offering of
your negative ego and mind to
the Lord and SatGuru
you are absorbed in His grace.
By heartful bhakti and by
offering your ego in the fire of
that devotion is
the ego dissolved.

"Interference of mind blocks the inflow of higher knowledge."

The word yoga is grossly misunderstood
to be physical asanas.
This is not so.
Yoga means Samadhi,
the ecstasy of
expanded consciousness.

There is a Pranayama where the
breath ceases spontaneously
while concentrating on an
external or internal object or
being absorbed deeply in something.

Concentration, dharana, is
exclusive attention.
It is binding the mind as a whole to
one single object.
Pulling your attention back
again and again to
that physical form of
the object each time it wanders
is called the
practice of concentration.

When you, the meditator, identify
yourself with the object of meditation
forgetting your own nature,
you have attained samadhi,
which is the ecstasy of expanded consciousness
beyond the vacillating thoughts and
disturbing emotions of the mind.

I fill the immensity of space –
I am the Self Supreme
Looking down I do perceive
creation as a dream.

The balance of the universe is rooted in reciprocity and the foundation of the evolution of the world is sacrifice

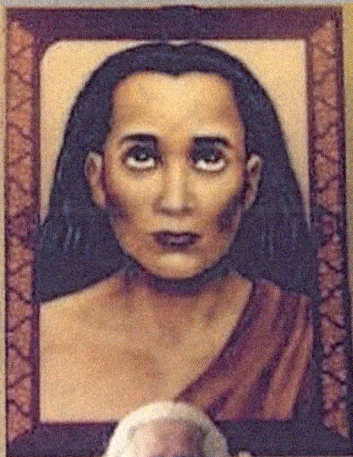

This knowledge is all supreme -
Its practice melts the magic dream.
Experience of the "Hamsa Still"
Makes Us know Divinity's will.

Om thou creative light divine
In all the seven heavens shine
Lightless light of all the light
Sun moon and fire you ignite

"Let not precious moments slip by.
Seek now, the ultimate truth."

Om with every breath & thought
Sets yogi free from karma
Giving Nirvana to striving souls
As per their own swadharms

Even the evil chanting 'Om'
Are tainted not by karma
They will be like a lotus lying
Unwet in water and undying

Deathless Yogi, fearless bold
Prana between the eyebrows hold
By kevali in Shivanetra be!
Oh death where is they victory?

Bring out your Hidden Power and lead yourself to enlightenment

In lotus posture yogi stay
Do sun-moon prana of night & day
Spinal breathing it is called
Victor of death be breath enthralled

He stands supreme beyond all dream
Of friend and foe alike
Success 'n failure, name and fame
To Him a mere dolls wedding game

BREATH
our uniting prayer

Satisfied with what he has
Bathing in wisdoms fountain head
Conqueror of the senses five
He drinks the honey from his hive

In joy and sorrow light & dark
He ever that eternal spark
In honor and dishonor too
The constant yogi ever new!

Beholding self by Self supreme
Shattering the waking dream
Maya shall be put to flight
By those who in the Self delight

"How shall I love Thee Babaji?
Words are so dry and dumb
I can't express Thy majesty
My intellect runs numb

....

I'm bursting in My love for Thee
Eternal Infinite
I cannot rest in peace now
Till I do become Thy Light..."

-Yogiraj Siddhanath

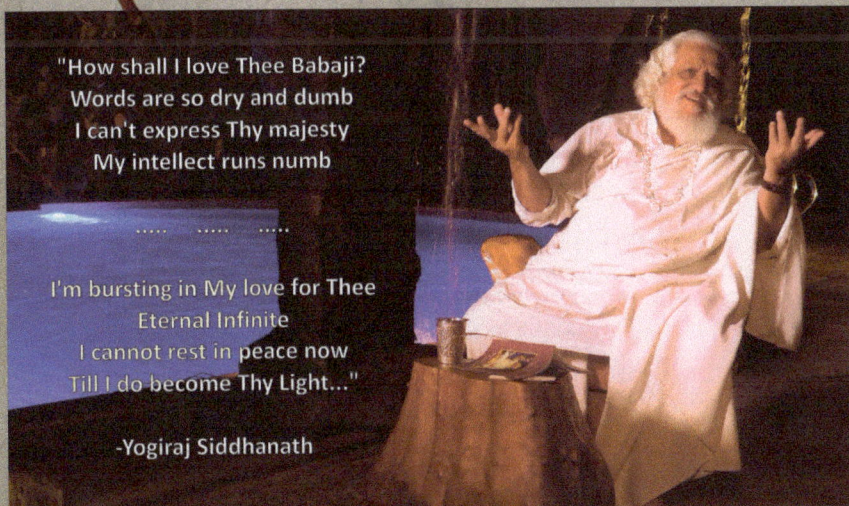

ACompassionate & healing light
A Hamsa in its splendid flight
Away oh darkness! Fly oh night!
The Yogi comes in radiant might.

W ho art Thou?
I know Thee not and yet I am of Thee
I cannot comprehend thee,
Oh Thou Emperor of Divinity.

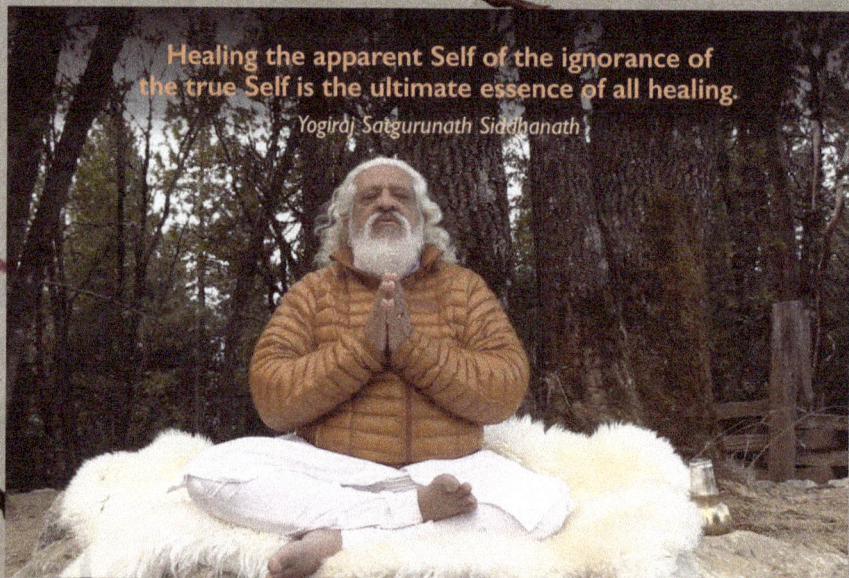

Healing the apparent Self of the ignorance of the true Self is the ultimate essence of all healing.

Yogiraj Satgurunath Siddhanath

I sit and melt in silence of
Thy Love Oh Infinite.
Make me thy Truth,
Make me thy Love
Eternal Lord of Light

The splendor of your Soul
is covered by the mud of the mind
which may be dissolved by
Spinal Breathing (Kriya Yoga)

I'm burning in My love for Thee
Eternal infinite
I cannot rest in peace now
Till I do become thy Light.

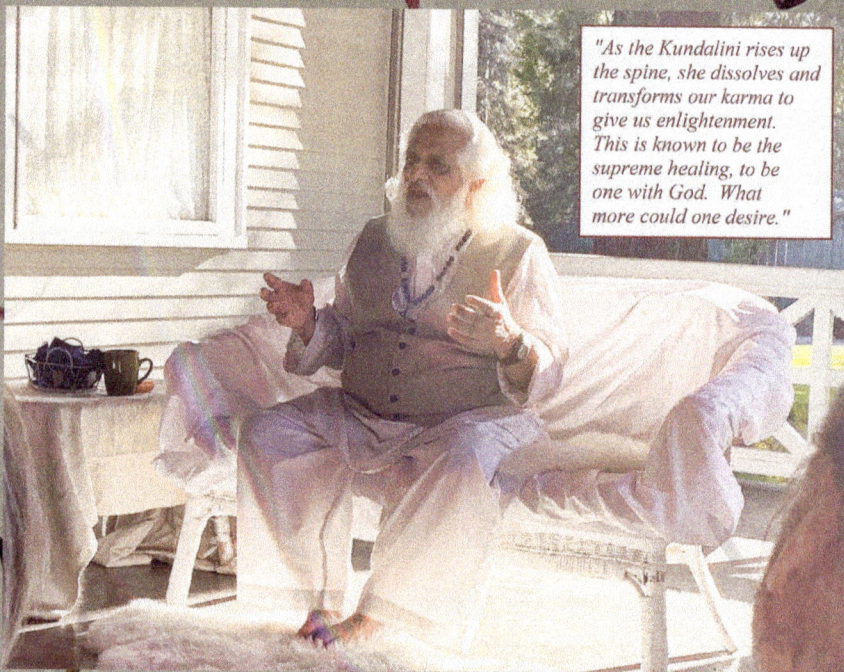

"As the Kundalini rises up the spine, she dissolves and transforms our karma to give us enlightenment. This is known to be the supreme healing, to be one with God. What more could one desire."

In silent supplications
I do burn and yearn to be in Thee
Hear Thou my soul cry
Break my bonds Babaji
Set me free.

When you, the meditator,
identify yourself with the object of meditation
forgetting your own nature,
you have attained samadhi,
which is the ecstasy of expanded consciousness
beyond the vacillating thoughts and
disturbing emotions of the mind.

*Climb up the
Spinal Staircase
of your consciousness...*

*Go and put on the lights...
and the darkness of the
subconscious mind
shall be not!*

Our minds to still
Meditation bring
Drink wisdom waters
Shasta spring

Your ability to realise the universe and then Reality, is a step by step progression, first by concentration, meditation, samadhi, then samyama, ranging from gross material objects to the subtler dimensions and finally pure Divine Consciousness.

Repeatedly holding on to that
thought-free moment of restraint,
a mind transformation occurs.
Each time you restrain the
cause from the effect,
this moment of restraint,
nirodha parinamah,
extends to longer periods
resulting in samadhi.

Then stiller than stillness itself
With bated breath, I do behold
My rising Self-Sun's nectar gold
I dissolve in that mystery untold.

This is it!
I've reached home.
I've quenched
the thirst of ages

Reality of
Kriya Yoga
is revelation of
Reality itself!

Yogi deathless, fearless bold, Prana between the eyebrows hold,
By kevali in Shiv Netra be! Oh death, where is thy victory?

Our nature has a common source,
the substratum of which is
dharmi gunas,
from which all latent manifest and
unmanifest properties of the mind arise;
the gunas are dormant, manifest and mixed.

Your mind flowing towards
the same object for 12 seconds
is concentration.
That mind continuing
concentration for 12 x 12 seconds
(2 minutes 24 seconds) is meditation.
The same mind continuing to
meditate for 12 x 2 minutes 24 seconds
(28 minutes 48 seconds) is
Samprajnata Samadhi.
Savikalpa Samadhi sustained for
12 times that period will
transcend the mind to expand into
the desireless consciousness of
Asamprajnata Samadhi or Nirvikalpa Samadhi.

Mindfulness is a focus of mind
which assists you to get to Soulfulness,
which merges into Conciousness,
the final Enlightenment.
In the state of Mindfulness a person's thoughts
are tutored and tuned by the
faculty of exclusive attention
to follow those train of thoughts,
uninterrupted by any other thought.

Specific traits that make an individual better suited for Kriya Yoga:

The first is humility.
The second is do not fault-find with others.
The third is unconditional love, Ishvar Pranidhan, towards the Master who awakens you – an offering of your heart and soul.
Then the last is you need concentrated persistence.
And that determination, that "fixity of purpose and flexibility of approach" is one of the great qualities that a devotee or traveller on the yogic path must have.

Soulfulness is a state of
effulgent intuitive Knowingness where the
undivided flow of your thoughts upon
a certain object becomes that object.
So deep is the state of absorption upon the
object that the mind forgets itself;
instead identifying totally with the object.

Conciousness is the final state of
Knowingness we call omniscience.
The association of your individual
Consciousness with your mind
purifies the mind to equal purity as your
Conciousness hence a merger takes place.
Your Consciousness taking along with it the
essence of mind merges into its own
unlimited Conciousness.

'When we go on to the more formidable aspects of Shakti, let us not for a moment forget, the spirit of love and the evolutionary push for the souls' salvation, which the Divine Mother has for us in her heart. Durga "the Unconquerable" is Adi Nath Shiva's consort in the aspect of warrior'.

~ Yogiraj SatGuruNath Siddhanath

Source: 'BABAJI The Lightning Standing Still'

Shiva is Babaji Gorksha
Sada Shiva is Mahadeva
Param Shiva is
REALITY

Meditation is the
effortless and unbroken state of concentration.
Here you do not have to struggle to keep your
attention focused on the single object because
extraneous thoughts occur less and are less
distracting, consequently it is easier for one
thought to flow across the mind's lake.

By samyama on
direct perception of the
latent impressions of the past,
you are blessed with the
knowledge of your previous births.

"Live your life like the Sun - incinerate your self to explode light and life to humanity."

By samyama on the
insight into another's perception,
you are blessed with
empathy of their mind and point of view.

Karma is divided into two portions:
prarabhda karma whose results are
already occurring and
sanchit karma,
actions whose fruits are yet to come.

Mind is the malady of humanity
and God is its remedy

Y ou gain all knowledge when
you develop the ability to
raise your centre of consciousness
up the central Sushumna channel,
through a flash of intuitive illumination or
pratibha effulgence.
Then, you will get all the facets of
supernormal divine siddhis.

By practicing samyama on
hridaya, the spiritual heart,
you will get complete knowledge of
the antakarna - mind, intellect, ego (asmita).

The mind and Atmic Seer are distinct.
The mind flows towards
sensual experience and
Atmic Seer exists in Itself.

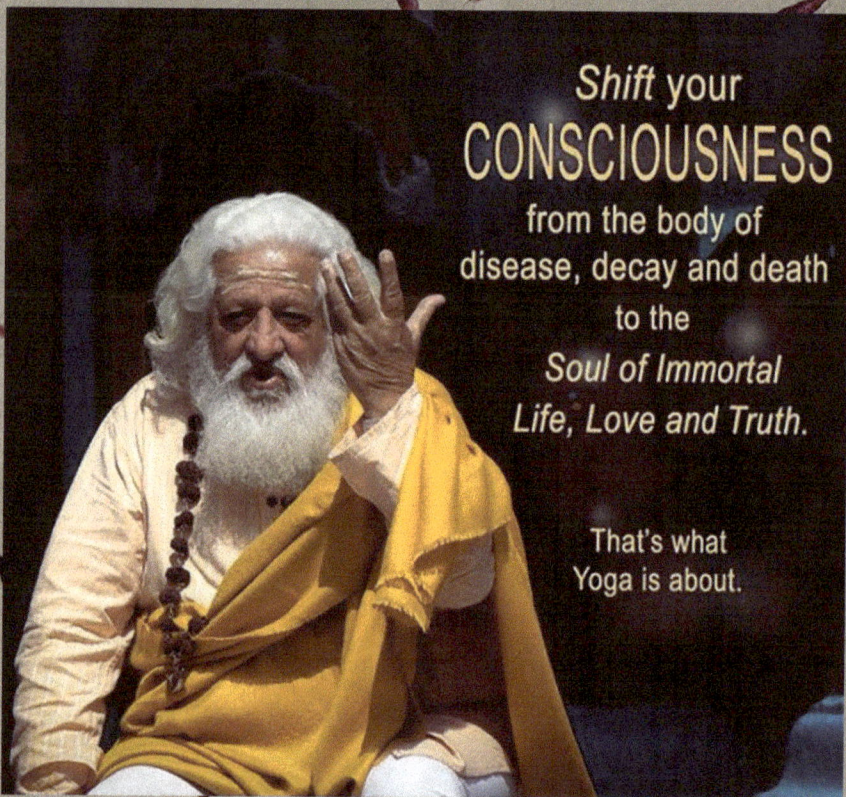

Shift your
CONSCIOUSNESS
from the body of
disease, decay and death
to the
Soul of Immortal
Life, Love and Truth.

That's what
Yoga is about.

These siddhis (psychic powers) are
obstacles to being absorbed in
spirit and attaining enlightenment.
Nevertheless they are seen as
attainments of perfection
to the worldly minded.

By the perfection of samyama on the
function of the senses,
you gain mastery of the senses
exploring all-pervasiveness and
yet remaining indifferent.
You, the Atmic Seer, know that
you are the
master of your senses and the mind

*"Babaji is the Spirit of Nothingness
whose peace
quenches the thirst of the ages."*

Only from the knowledge of the distinction between the mind, your apparent self and identification with Consciousness, your true Self, comes the omniscience and supremacy over all the states and manifestations of the mind.

By non-attachment to omniscience and even
to buddhic wisdom comes the
burning of the seeds of bondage
in all their totality.
Then the great veil of maya, delusion,
gives way to the dawn of the
Supreme Reality, Kaivalya.

When the light of divine mind
becomes equal in purity to your
Divine Consciousness, then by the
Gravitas of your Consciousness,
the divine mind is transformed and
absorbed into Divine Consciousness,
to merge in Kaivalya.

Offer the inhaled into the exhaled breath
and the exhaled into the inhaled breath

Occasionally a siddha is born
amongst normal people to help their evolution.
His supernatural powers result from
five past life karmic mindsets:
exalted birth, magical herbs, mantra,
austere practices, absorption, samadhi.

By the positive force of nature and the
momentum of past life practices,
you evolve from birth to birth,
purifying your mind into effulgent light,
then transforming yourself into an Immortal.

One with Shiva I have become
All my attachments are broken
And One with Shiva I have become

Just as a farmer removes the
obstacles from irrigation ditches in his field
allowing the clogged water to flow,
so the trap door of the mind is opened by
yoga practice, enabling Self-consciousness
to flow into
Universal Consciousness

A perfected yogi is neither affected by
good or bad karma.
But for normal people their actions are of
three kinds: good, bad and mixed, which
create karma.
The yogi's actions
do not produce any karma.

Karma manifest when conditions are
favourable for ripening.
Other tendencies remain dormant to
manifest in some future birth when
circumstances are favourable.
Hence this sutra refers to the
karma of non-yogis

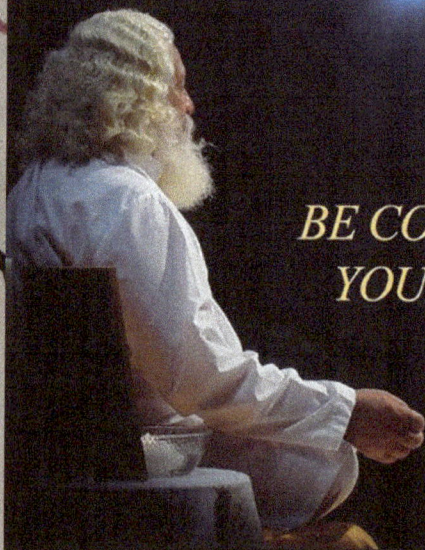

YE SONS OF LIGHT
DELUSION FIGHT

BE CONSTANT IN
YOUR DAY AND NIGHT

The primal desire to live moves the
world cycle and the law of karma that
produces rebirth in order to
connect cause to effect.
The current of passions to live
flows from animals right up to the human race.
This is because memory, smriti, and
impressions, samskara, are without beginning.

The way to end the cycle of cause and effect that produce pleasure and pain, death and rebirth is by disconnecting cause from effect by, for example, disconnecting the senses from their objects, memory from latent impressions and Consciousness from the mind through samadhi.

"The intake of my every breath, I drink as amrit of thy love.
And let that nectar mix, in every atom of my blood."

Mind contains within it in
potential form all mental characteristics
manifest in the past and those which can
manifest in the future.
Because of the law of cause and effect, karma,
the characteristics that will arise to
become visible in the future will
depend upon the path you travel in the present.

Though the essence of the object
remains the same,
owing to the differences in the mind,
people have distinctly different
perceptions of the same object

When the mind is receptive and
allows itself to be colored by the object,
by that color is that object known or unknown.
Otherwise, while the object may be in
front of you, if your mind is
engrossed elsewhere,
even with open eyes
you will not see it.

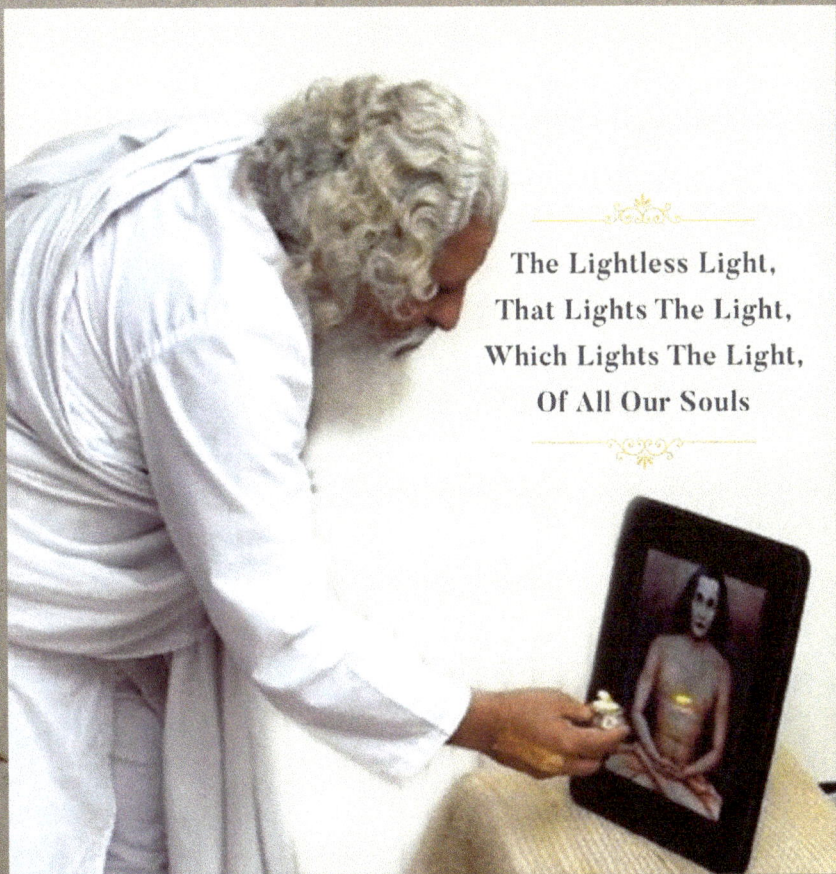

The Lightless Light,
That Lights The Light,
Which Lights The Light,
Of All Our Souls

Mind is an object that cannot
illuminate itself.
As the moon shines in the borrowed light of
the sun, so our mind, but a
tool of cognition, cognizes in the
borrowed light of the Atma.

The mind itself is an object and
an instrument of knowing; and
therefore cannot comprehend
both subject and object simultaneously

**FORGET THE PAST
IT IS DEAD AND GONE**

*FROM MOMENT TO MOMENT, I AM BORN ANEW...
IN EVERY BREATH, I AM PURE...
IN EVERY BREATH, I AM BORN ANEW.*

This world our sages did perceive as
mindstuff materialized
In relative sequence it has been
deceiving mortal eyes

Samadhi is a natural state of enlightenment.
When the Consciousness enters
different sheaths of the body,
there is a descent of this state of awareness
into grosser and grosser sheaths.

So the breath is infused into the flesh
with such force that
you think you are the body,
whereas you are actually the Soul.
And yoga is a technique to reverse the
electrical flow of prana, to
regain paradise lost.

You are a Soul,
and have a body.

What is the purpose of the soul
incarnating into
denser spheres of consciousness?
The only limited answer or partial answer
you could find to this,
is to gain experience in the material world.
The soul gains its experience of joy and sorrow,
light and dark, bad and good in
this world of relativity.
Nothing is actually bad and good –
it's all relative.

The urge is to go back to your parent source
- in the beginning, there was the
Absolute Stillness, the silence of the
Seven Eternities - profound, the
Great Fathomless Deep,
which was so essential and
truthful in its nothingness that out of it
everything came.

I fill immensity of space –
I am the Self Supreme
Looking down I do perceive
creation as a dream

Then there was the
primordial explosion of the Great Bang, the
sound of Aum,
the light sound explosion of
billions and trillions of supernovae -
a supernovae nuclear explosion of
inconceivable proportions whose
sound is resonating after billions of years
even today, which is forming our creation and
giving birth to life on this planet,
all species including man,
by the virtue of the sound called Aum.

Now when the drop merges into the Ocean,
it does merge its individual identity into the
Cosmic Identity but it does not lose
its identity. Keeping its identity, it partakes -
this is the other half of the truth -
it does not lose its identity,
the drop merging into the Ocean.
It merges into the Ocean but
it partakes of the identity,
it partakes of the Awareness of the Ocean.
So you do not become lost unto yourself but
you expand into a Divine Consciousness.

So have no fear,
take the leap.
Dive headlong into the
Divine experience of samadhi and
live on, for
you shall be yourself and
much, much more.

I then blend in the everlasting
vast expanse of Light
Becoming one with the
Cosmic Hum of all resounding Om.

Wexml are all like icebergs
floating on the ocean.
But when the Sun of Knowledge arises,
we melt our individual ego identities and
merge into the
One Consciousness of the Ocean.

Then tamed and tuned to Nature's flow
Mind melts into the opal glow
Radiating from the Soul within
Where Wisdom's mystic fire is King

One thought of immortality
affects the thought of the whole world

So there's no causation, space nor time
in the house of God
There is Nothing
Causation, Space and time break away

Ultimately just as Eternity and Infinity
meet at the same point because
they are both infinite,
the empty and full are both the same.
So what do we say for the state of the
Complete Absolute,
if from the Complete Absolute state,
the complete and absolute are taken out?
The Complete Still remains complete.

It is the experience of
God's own Truth within the
depths of your own consciousness
to feel the indwelling Shiva,
to feel the indwelling Buddha,
this is what is important and
this is the ultimate medicine
to cure all your maladies and all your disease.

Become a flame unto yourself
Become a light unto yourself
Don't live on borrowed light
Become your own light
Don't depend on me
Depend on God
Depend utterly upon yourself
No other dependence
No shelter anywhere
No refuge

The greatest healing,
the greatest medicine, is
to heal the apparent self of
the ignorance of the True Self,
by removing the thoughts.
So stilling the mind when
you are in the Void or Emptiness.

Who art Thou
I know Thee Not
Yet I am of Thee
I cannot comprehend Thee Lord
Emperor of Divinity

So I sit and melt in silence
Of Thy Love Oh Infinite
Make me Thy Truth
Make me Thy Love
Oh Lord of light

THE SOUND OF SILENCE
WILL WASH AWAY THE MUD
OF THE MIND THAT COVERS
THE SPLENDOR OF YOUR SOUL

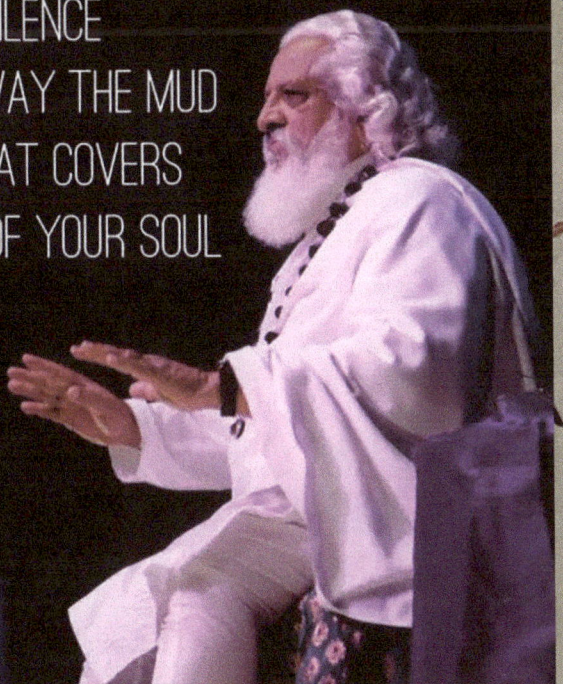

Babaji
is
The Heart of Divinity
Throbbing in Humanity

Fact becomes history,
History becomes legend,
Legend becomes myth,
And myth rxperienced becomes fact.
This is the truth of the turning wheel of time
Called the Kaal Chakra

Boundless lay the Self in the
Knowingness of Itself,
Spread beyond infinity, from
eternity to eternity,
was perfect absolute and calm;
calm undisturbed,
for Creation was not yet
conceived of the Creator.

"This world is but a thoughtfulness of mayic atoms intertwined, whose electrons are energy of light essence sublime."

Absolute perfection art thou
Oh All-in-All,
Not this, nor that art thou,
the essence of light and dark,
There was no darkness then,
there even was no light
There was no action then to cause reaction,
all was thy ineffable and
endless consciousness of Bliss

If at one moment, time and place,
The sunburst of a countless suns occur.
That brilliance would scarce suffice
to show Thy shadow
Oh Lord, what must be Thy Light!

"To transmute the minds of sincere seekers of yoga into a higher state of consciousness is the purpose of my work."

Lo! Thou didst exhale Thy universal Self,
Oh Calm
And Thy Infinite Mind did make the mighty
Lord of Flame
Who exploding in His Light did
Maya's Creation ignite
To set the wheel of causation and
relativity in motion,
Creating the law of Karma,
Dharma & Reincarnation.

The eternal Mother Adi-Shakti
then did make her galaxies
And other relative aspects of creation
did begin,
Light-Sound sublime,
created causation space and time
Originating in Thy
transcendental matrix of light
Resounding in every atom of creation,
Thy organ Omm!

These mighty vapors of jeweled-light
they stud Thy brow
Of Thou Mother of Eternity
Thy glory knows no night
These children galaxies of Thine,
Stellar Solar systems hold;
By that force we mortals call
Thy gravitational love,
In perfect harmony their
cosmic dance unfolds.

232

Live your life with absolute fixity of purpose and absolute flexibility of approach.

Oh Mother nurturer, by whose womb
we mortals were born,
Our endless salutations to Thee.
Oh Thou Divine spouse of the
great preserver, Vishnu.
Our Universe of Endless stars
lives their lives in Thee
Only so long as
Thou dost wish them to be.

The Earth was born from the watery space,
Which was born of the Solar essence,
Whose original source was the
fabric of radiant ether,
Known as Padma-Matrika,
meaning the Lotus Mother,
Who was essentially of Brahma,
the Creator.

"If you dwell on the thought of light and love, then light and love shall be your outcome."

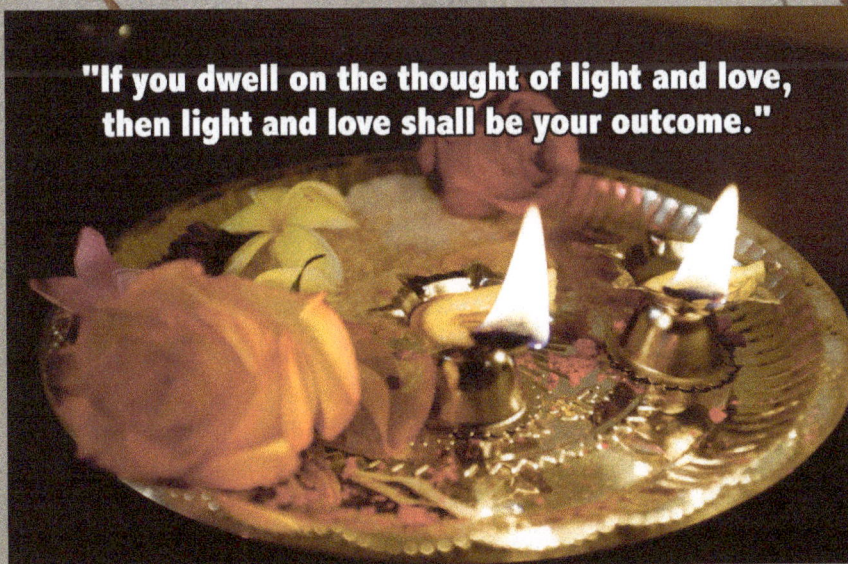

The group Soul spark
grew from the mineral rock,
Into the plant, wherein it did flourish.
Dying out from the plant the Spark of life
Was born into the fish and then the mammals.
Migrating from the lower form
to a more expressive one.

I died out from the rock to live in the plant.
I died out from the plant to
live in the fish and reptile.
Then live in animal form and
lastly enter the house of man,
Wherein did I become the lesser by dying?
For dying was only another form of life.

And all along Evolution's path did I travel,
My outer coats are more
expressive than the former,
But essentially I was the same.
And finally awaited me the temple of Man
But it was only a man of clay,
until I entered my ray.

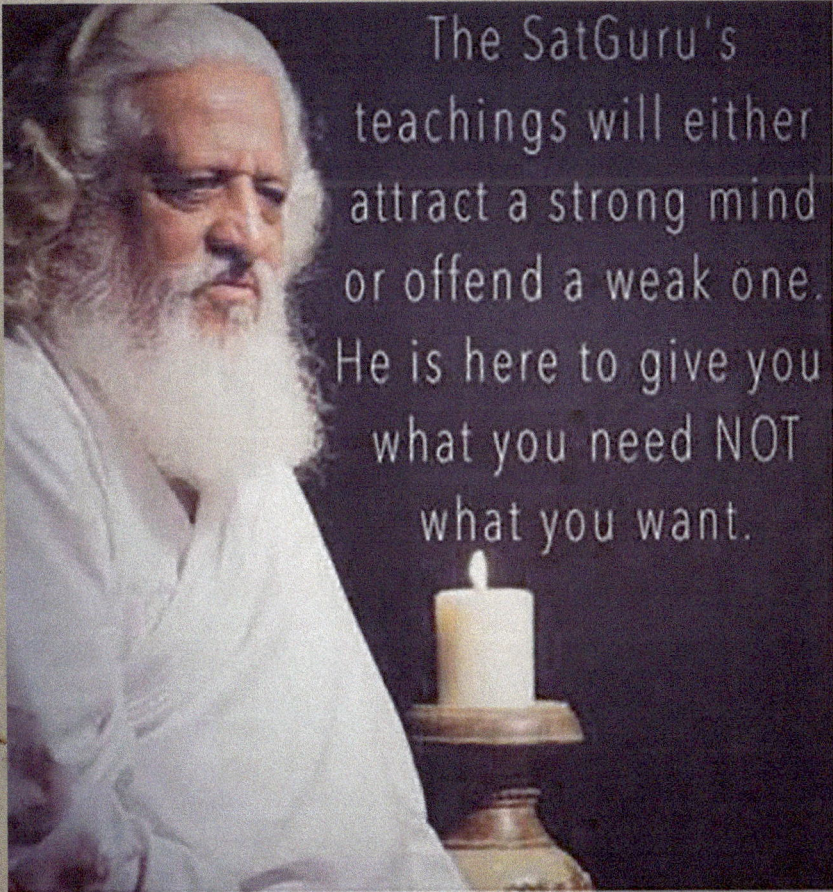

The SatGuru's teachings will either attract a strong mind or offend a weak one. He is here to give you what you need NOT what you want.

I entered into man as ray of thinking light,
I was that consciousness of Supreme delight.
I gave the house of flesh to know
I was the child of light.
The Ego it was formed by me
for future generations to be
The delusive "I" of the mind,
the segregator of all Mankind.

I came into the physical house of man,
To rule over that Tabernacle of the body,
But was deluded by the
Satanic desires of the Flesh
Into thinking I was a body and not
the knowing light.
This Heresy of separateness
covered my sight.

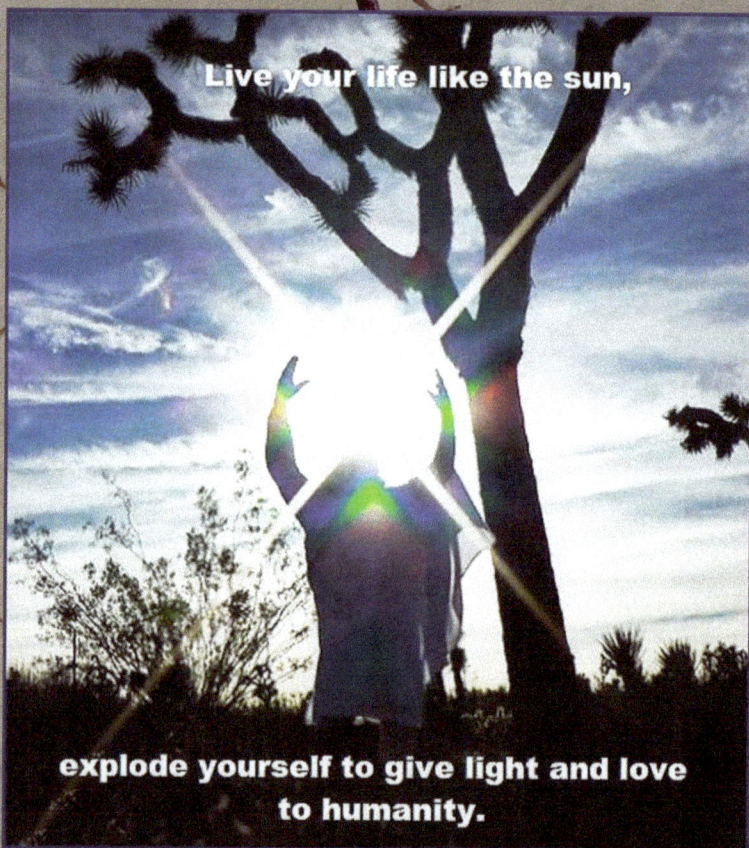

Live your life like the sun, explode yourself to give light and love to humanity.

Forgetting I was potentially Divine,
Illusive Maya's veil covered my Soul spark
Separating me from my True identity
To tempt me by the sensual life
And haunt me in the darkness of body flesh.

Then man looked up to the portending stars
to question whether they his life did make.
The stars replied
"Nothing can Thy Immortal Essence take."
Then girding up His Loins,
the human did begin
His upward evolution striving
to be the Divine within.

Thou nature's eve, Thou didst
hide my thinking Self
From my Father the Spirit Self within.
Evolution began to unite
The thinking Self that was me to me
Father Divinity and a free Soul to be;
then the Self began its
rounds of cyclic evolution.

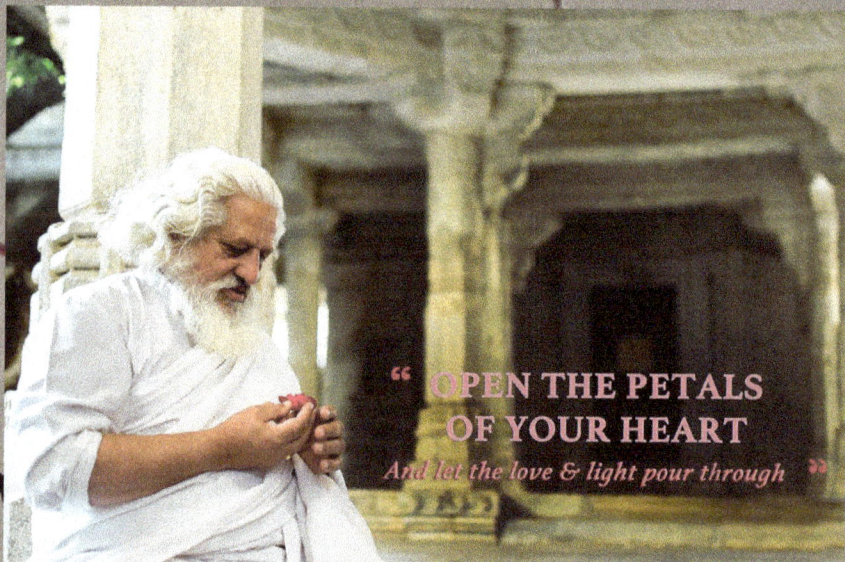

" OPEN THE PETALS
OF YOUR HEART
And let the love & light pour through "

It persevered until the mind-Self
Defeated the passional ego-Self
To become one with the
higher mind intelligence
Then unite with Atma, the inner knower,
Who one was with the Universal Knower

The Father Spirit, the Mother Intelligence
And Mind-Child had become one.
Lo! The deluded Mind-Child
Had regained His lost birthright and
Entered into the Father-Mother bosom of Light.

"Sacrifice is the highest love "

The fallen state regained: Lo!
Behold the lesser ones to come.
The lower animals had to struggle up.
Oh Sons of light help them! Guide them!
The plants, the rocks must be evolved too.

For in all is the essential spark of Atman.
The Cosmic Divine Self must
Help the individual human Self.
This is the Divine decree promulgated
by Babaji
Who is called Mahabinishkaran,
the Great Sacrifice.

The molecules in each
mineral substance did contain
Vast quantity of atoms,
each representing
A miniature Solar System
revolving and evolving
Powered by the compassion of Babaji,
our revered Father
Who is the ineffable Cosmic essence of the
Self Atma.

Y ou are not alone
for I am here with you.

His Spirit is the essence of All,
both big and small,
Hot and cold, light and dark, doth contain
That one essential spark,
The electrons in its essence
Positrons that were composed of
mesons whose energy
Lifetrons traveled through the
breath of man.

But finer than the lifetrons of Prana was the
Essence of God-thought,
One with the all-pervading Spirit, the Atman.
There was no segregation in this
Spirit of God-thought,
For from this was the
dream fabric of Creation composed.
This was the vastest
infinity of manifest Divinity.

Man has three layers in his being:
knowing, feeling, and doing.

The paths of Gyana yoga: the path of knowledge,
Bhakti yoga: the path of devotion and
Karma yoga: the path of action
evolved because of these three layers.

Intellect and knowledge knows
but cannot feel or do
Emotions feel but don't know or do
Actions can do but cannot know or feel.

Thus man is stuck in the triangle of action,
knowledge, and feeling.

Kriya is the only technique that integrates all
into one unity.
That's the genius of Shiva Goraksha Babaji.

From the essential substance of God thought
the Sun and the Moon and the Stars were built,
Stella and Solar Systems also had their sway
because God thought was in them to stay.
All was God thought, God thought was
One thought,
The divine thought of the
universal oneness of Eternity.

For being the subtlest of the all from it was
made the all;
It was the smallest of the small
far beyond human imagination.
Would it then be correct to call that
God-thought non-Being?
And thereby express its
absolute entirety over
creation in Being?

The All-being was the
God-thought which was
Babaji the essential Self,
of every atom of creation.
The Self that all pervading consciousness
Of stillness through
eternity composed of nothing
yet of which all else is sure composed,
It stands supreme beyond
all dreams eternally reposed.

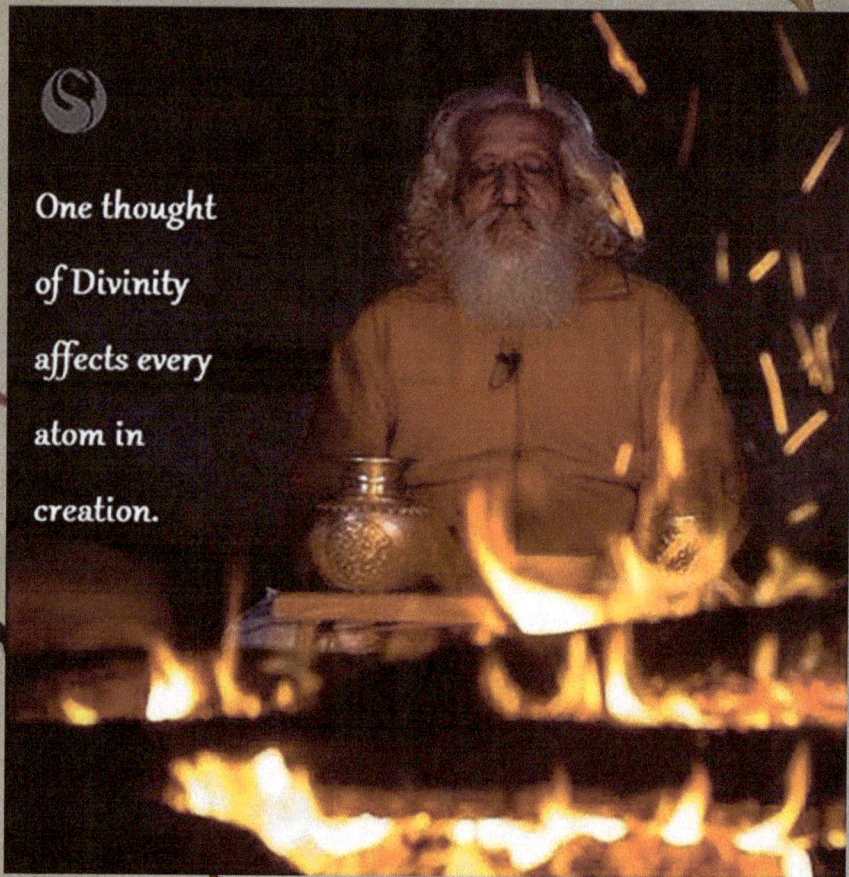

One thought
of Divinity
affects every
atom in
creation.

Spirit is the God-thought,
there is nothing it is not.
The All is One, the One is all,
the All-in All Paramartha
Oh, Absolute Majesty of sublimest existence,
Oh ineffable peace
beyond human understanding,
Our ceaseless salutation to Thee
who ever was, even is now and
shall forever be.

If I could but with Time conspire
To relive my past life movie entire
Fashioning my future picture show
In tune with God's own mystic flow

My only prayer is this:
"Allow me to be alert wherever I am.
Let me be fully aware wherever I am."

You see, where you are,
whether it is hell or heaven,
that is irrelevant . . .
because if you are fully alert in the moment,
Hell disappears - Hell is your being not aware.
If you are fully aware in the moment,
Heaven appears - Heaven is your being fully aware.

As the steward of the Cosmos from age to age,
it is Shiva Goraksha Babaji who undertakes the
task of guarding the seeds of Creation
through the birth, destruction, and
rebirth of each of the created universes.
Each universe comes into being
with a tremendous light-sound explosion known
as The Big Bang where,
within a billionth of a second,
matter expands in all directions at
an inconceivable velocity
to form the phenomena called Creation.
This is called the
"sound of the instant creation."
The Omkar.

The kundalini is intensified spiritual prana.
If the pranic energy is to be compared to the
atomic bomb, the voltage of the kundalini
energy benefits the guided yogi like a
benevolent hydrogen bomb.
The kundalini shakti (force) is activated
and awakened during the Kriya Yoga pranayama,
which I call the kundalini breath.
It is hidden and latent within all human beings in
their nervous system.

Oh Divine Guru, Supreme Guru,
show us the path.
We drink thy essence of joy,
we drink the golden radiance,
and let Thy solar gold
go up and down our spine,
to evolve us through
the years of our cycles.

The "Prana" is where the "Chitta" is.
Prana and mind (Chitta) have the
relationship of the supporter and the supported.
Like the rose and its perfume.

One ceases to exist without the other.
If the Mind is controlled,
then the Prana is controlled.
Prana flows where the mind is guided to.

He is the head, the heart, the seed and the
Soul of undying Knowledge
spread from Infinity to Infinity
beyond the Seven Eternities.
He is the Lightening Standing Still.
He is the Nameless One
who broods over humanity
for eons of millions of years.

Oh Lord, let us think of Thee
While we take every morsel of food
Let us think of Thee
Let us not think of food as things
to eat but as thy food
Let us think of it as a spiritual act
Thou art the food, the eater and digester
May this food give us the good sense
to worship thee
And love thee.

All you have to do is be aware
when breath comes in - "Ham"
when the breath leaves - "Saa"
If you go on practicing breathing like this,
breathing with awareness,
one day, without knowing,
you will come to the interval
between the outgoing breath
and the incoming breath . . .   this where you enter
into a different consciousness
You will realize
"THAT"
which is neither born nor dies
You will know that
eternal element which always
"IS"

If at one moment time and place,
the sun burst of a countless suns occurred,
this would scarce suffice to show thy shadow.
Oh lord what must be thy light.

Deathless splendor fearless bold
Goraksha the living lightning holds
Savior of gods and human kind
Liberates them from the karmic grind

The son of Shiva and Parvati
Goraksha in Ganesha Goshti
Being Shiva himself in formless form
Taught Ganesha Samadhi of Divinity

Live God, Love God,
Die God, Be God,
God God, God God,
God God, God God

From Your sacred fire did You take
The potent ashes of Your Dhuni
And gave it to Vishnu and Brahma
Creation to again remake

Y ou battled the Goddess of Hingalaaja
And freed her from mayic mirage
To Datta you gave his mantra as draum
Enlightened him to its origin from Om

Dissolve the whirlpool of the mind.
What remains is You.

Hanumana and Bhima at territory war
You pacified both and settled the score
First testing Arjuna by killing the boar
Then gifting him with the Gandiva bow

To Mary the gift of Christ You bestowed
In Gabriel's apparel You were clothed
It is written in the books of Dabisthana
To the Prophet You gave knowledge of gyana

Shiva born the disciple of Macchendra yogi
Took the name of Goraksha Mahayogi
Steered Macchendra off the mayic tryst
Illumined and melted his karmic mist

In the state of passive awareness
you need no Bhakti, no Shakti,
just be

Desires for golden palace by Bharthari
You fulfilled in the incarnation of Lahiri
Chowringee disciple of Goraksha Ishwara
Reincarnated as Yogi Yukteshwar

The glories of Krishna did Meera sing
But her life and living to Goraksha bring
He did Alam Prabhu's ignorance efface
And showed to him Goraksha's God-own face

There is God in man,
when you breathe the man,
God will manifest

Kabir was born as Yogi Sri Chandra
Then Lahiri the conqueror of Indra
Vikramaditya was your disciple true
Born as Siddhanath Kriya work to do

To Ramananda the joy of Rama you gave
To Kabir the Kriya Yoga of prana
To Nanak you gave the true Sat-nam
Irradiant Lord beyond death and grave

The king of mystics was Gyannath
Initiated by brother Nivrittinath
Who in turn was blessed by Gahninath
Your kundalini disciples on yogic path

In giving out my breath,
I sacrifice to thee: my health, my happiness,
my prana;
all at thy Lotus Feet

In Gorakpur was Yogananda born
He was chosen for the yogic norm
Sent by Sri Yukteshwar to the west
To spread Kriya Yoga and to do his best

Ye sons of light
Delusion fight
Be constant in
Your day and night

When the Soul is burned with
the fire of devotion,
the perfume is nectarine

Countless creations do you make
Goraksha Nath Divine
A thought projected by you
Makes causation, space and time

There never was a Sage or Saint
Who was not born of Thee
Thou art the essence of their Souls
Divine Paramatma Free

We Jivatmas also Lord
Have our birth and being in Thee
Then Thou must also be in us
Supremest Monarchy

That which exists after everything ceases
is the everlasting Reality which
people call by many names
yet is called The Nameless One

How shall I love Thee Babaji?
Words are so dry and dumb
I can't express Thy majesty
My intellect runs numb

My heart it bursts oh all in all
To love Thee endlessly
But Lord I cannot bring to words
I'm tongue-tied hopelessly

W hat is the garbage which covers
the Splendor of your soul?
It is your thoughts.

Give me the strength to shout Thy love
Across the seven seas
Deludging this world with light
For infinite eternities

300

In solitudes of my mind
My devotion it dost burst to hear
Thy song immortal song of love
Thou everlasting Seer

As long as darkness covers me
And ignorance doth do us part
So long in agony I'll be
Striving to be with Thee, my Heart

Kriya Yoga dehypnotizes you
into realizing that
you are a divine soul
not a corruptible body

Through pain and hunger I shall strive
To touch Thy feet oh Lord
It matters not if bones or body
Perish in this battle fort

I'm burning in My love for Thee
Eternal Infinite
I cannot rest in peace now
Till I do become thy Light

Live your life like an incense stick –
dissolve yourself to spread
peace and joy to those you serve

In silent supplications
I do burn and yearn to be in Thee
Hear Thou my soul cry
Break my bonds, Babaji set me free

S et me free to be in Thee
Let there be none of me
Then me in Thee, Thy love in me
I shall become of Thee

Living in Calm and Solitude
Subduing body and his Mind
Within himself in gratitude
Ridding Desires of all Kind.

The only purpose of man's sojourn
on this earth is
to seek God

'Neath Sylvan bowers in his Seat
Cool Stream flows by deerskin laid neat
This is the Yogi's true retreat
In meditation is his treat.

The Asans selected best are two
For him to meditation do
The first Padmasana lotus trance
Then Siddhasana the perfect stance.

If we go deep into the meaning of Guru:
Gu is derived from Guhya which means
"hidden knowledge of spiritual gravity" and
Ru means "light of knowingness"
so the Satguru is "he who brings to light
the gravity of God inherent to Man"

Y ogi's in Dhyan become aware
How breath at birth did them ensnare
Twenty one thousand thirty score
Japa leads soul to salvation's door.

In Padmasan do bandh trine
Focus on Kundalini in spine
Practice breathing Pran-apan
Know precious Kundalini Gyan.

Food is energy for the mind
And goes to mental making
Soft sweets and fruits oh! Yogi eat
At every fast of breaking

Always remember this: I am Spirit,
I am Truth, I am Love Divine.
This body mind a dream of mine.

For psychic nerves to Purify
One must move both sun and moon
And all humours is us to dry
We must perfect maha-mudra try

Hamsa is Gayatri's ajapa japa
Opener of Yogi's heavenly door
Breathing with awareness let him strive
And let not him his animal drive

The Universe a bubble in my consciousness
my consciousness a nothing in Thy Nothingness

From Kundali is Hamsa born
Flowing in spine as Pran-apan
Yogi's stilling the Pran-apan
Are true adepts in sama Dhyan.

Oh valiant Yogi striving free
By pranic kumbak break the seal
The Brave by storm the heaven's take
Nirvan through kundali they make

Having blocked with her face
The path leading to Shiva's shrine
Awake! Oh Kundalini mine
And lead me to my home divine!

Practice of the Kriya free
Is Soul's journey to reality
One with your True Self to be

The Yogic Prana ablaze unites
With Kundalini to ignite
Mind intellect then penetrate
Sukhma chakras living light

She like a hissing serpent goes
Glistening kundali upward flows
By magnet heat of Pranayam
Awaken's she! Our wisdom grows

As the gentle abrasion of a river
transforms a rough stone
into a rounded Shivalinga, so,
the gentle abrasion of the Kriya breath
transforms every Jiva into Shiva!

Y our own meat swallow yogi
Get drunk with inner wine
The profane value these secrets not
Cast not your pearls before the swine

By Allakh Gorakhias mystic touch
Disease hunger not sleep assail
Yogis who rent mayas death veil
Are those who in khechari prevail

By afflictions is he troubled not
Nor tainted by his fruits of karma
Is troubled not by sting of death
He Mirtyunjay conqueror of breath

But Deathlessnes to me
is naught unless
Divinity's Light shines forth

Om thou creative light divine
in all the seven heavens shine
Lightless light of all the light
Sun moon and fire you ignite

In the Blueprint of creation
Emblazoned is thy cosmic seal
Causation space & time are but
Projections of your magic dream

Not for the sake of deathlessness
but for the sake Divine
I transform immortality
by Awareness to Divinity!

Om with every breath & thought
Sets yogi free from karma
Giving Nirvana to striving souls
As per their own swadharms

Absorbed in Om, the semen stills
By ceaseless Pranayama
Lifeprana is still, semen is still
Conquer death, new life fulfill

As long as pran in body flows
The soul therein doth reside
Pran leaves, soul also body leaves
So live for God! Do Pranayam

You are all
Children of the Lord.
Blessed are you.

To ward off kala death they say
Gods and sages in Pranayam stay
Yogi puts deaths fear away
And lives in prana the kevali way

He stands supreme beyond all dream
Of friend and foe alike
Success 'n failure, name and fame
To Him a mere dolls wedding game

340

While experiencing the various stages of
spiritual awareness,
one has to be true to oneself.

Remember . . . that the great sages, alive
through the ages, can see through the hearts
and minds of humanity.

They know exactly where each individual
stands in the hierarchy of his personal
evolution and the depth of his devotion
to God.

Satisfied with what he has
Bathing in wisdoms fountain head
Conqueror of the senses five
He drinks the honey from his hive

Established in the Self he glows
Beyond intelligence he flow's
Transcending all the senses five
In the "here-now!" Truth alive

Beholding self by Self supreme
Shattering the waking dream
Maya shall be put to flight
By those who in the Self delight

Alchemy of Total Transformation

Rub the Tinder, Fire Manifests
Churn the Milk, Butter Manifests
Breathe the Man, God Manifests!

A Compassionate & healing light
A Hamsa in its splendid flight
Away oh darkness! Fly oh night!
The Yogi comes in radiant might.

Niyam, Yama discipline
the conduct of a person
Asanas discipline the body
Pranayama purifies the emotions
Dharana shapes the mind.
Dhyana furthers the Awareness of Mind
Samadhi "Is" the ecstasy of
expanded consciousness

Yoga is the practice of absorption
of Soul into Spirit,
whereby
Sorrow and Desire creating Karma dissolve
consequently
Freeing one's soul bound
to the Cycle of Birth and Death
giving it
the Final Liberation - Niranjana - Nirvana

Kriya Yoga is an inner ascent
through ever
more refined,
and ever more expanded spheres
of mind,
to get to that Consciousness
which lies at the core of our own being.

An experience of union with life
is not possible
where there is nonacceptance of
life's conditions;
a resentful wish to be otherwise
or have otherwise or an attitude to things
and people as they are.

The Yogi has to be so intent upon the creation
of a new self that he has no leisure for
grumbling at his environment.

Babaji The Lightless Light
Doth Shine Upon The Horsemens' Flight
Compassionate and Healing Lights
Four Horsemen In Their Splendid Flights
Away Oh Darkness Fly Oh Night
The Yogis Come In Radiant Might

Birth and Death are a chapter
in your life story,
but you as the immortal
River of Livingness
Flow On!

The mind is the
shadow of the Soul
and the shadow of
the mind is the body.
At death you just
cast away the body
and you take
another body.
Forget the fear of
death and strive
wholeheartedly
to realize the
Divinity within.

The Ultimate Healing is Realizing God
The Ultimate Magic is Knowing God
The Ultimate Yoga is Becoming God

Hiss Kundali sting ego mine
With nectar poison so sublime
Piercing my rainbow Lotus shrines
Making me to myself divine !

From the Guru's feet flows
the spiritual river Ganga
which washes all the sins of my heart.
Oh Shiva, when will my relationship
with you become one?

Kundalini bless me with thy blaze
Delusion, suffering fear efface
Spine darkness; with thy lightening light
Fragrance me ! Negative karma ignite !

Y ou are livingness ! its Life you keep
Oh Mother of the mystic deep !
Remove shadow of death from me
In Shiva deathlessly to be !

Just as gold when heated (tapa)
comes clear of the slag
shining in its pristine purity
so Jivatma by Tapa of Pranayama
is cleansed of vishaya vasana
and shines in its pristine glory!!

Outside the Temple of Zeus
Awareing the Guardian Wall of Humanity
He will not quit his Watch till
the last disciple is Free!

Who feels Thy love Beloved Christ,
it spreads into eternity
It permeates each atom our existing Humanity.
Each fibre in my body and
my innermost spirit yearns for Thee
In what fashion shall I Lord!
Express my burning love for Thee.

God is not a goal:
God is what is
here and now

The undifferentiated consciousness of the master gravitates itself into the light-mind existence of the thought-mind of the seeker, thus transforming the seeker's mind to his own consciousness; to the degree of the attunement of that mind with the Master's consciousness.

~Yog~Martand Yogiraj Siddhanath

www.siddhanath-india.org

Speak to me Jesus in my heart and
tell me Thou art mine.
Such is the depth and warmth of
Thy ineffable love divine.
Speak to me Jesus in my heart and
tell me thou art mine.
Tell me Oh Christ; That I am Thine
I ask for nothing more

Oh King of Yogis little did
these blinded children know
That Thou were master of Thy body and
its passing show!
Then brighter than brilliance itself
on Easter Thou didst rise
To show the Light of love divine to
blinded mortal eyes.

The Krishna and the Christ perceived
light to be form of energy.
Emanating from the omniscient mind
that one cosmic reality.

They further saw that energy
was not the final law.
It was a grosser consciousness
but that too had its flaw.

This world our sages did perceive
is mindstuff materialized.
In relative sequence it is built
deceiving mortal eyes.

Oh! Supreme Guru of the nature of bliss,
Sanctify and make my heart full of joy.
Thou art knowledge personified,
full of Spirit and essence of truth,
make me unto Thy likeness
Thou King of Yogis who
dispels negativity and disease,
embodiment of Enlightenment and Peace.
To such a Divine Guru, my ceaseless salutations.

Yogiraj SatGurunath Siddhanath
A brief introduction to his teachings

His Life

Yogiraj Sat Gurunath was born on May 10th, 1944. He is a Siddha by birth and belongs to one of the premier families of Gwalior, India. Educated in Sherwood College [Nainital], he spent his early years in the Himalayas with the great Nath Yogis, in whose presence he was transformed. The Divine Transformation was completed by his deep and personal experience with Mahavtar Babaji (Shiva-Goraksha-Nath Babaji) – the same immortal introduced by Yogananda in his classic, 'Autobiography of a Yogi'. Yogiraj is a direct disciple of Babaji and with his blessings has founded the Siddhanath Yoga Parampara.

Yogiraj now teaches various ancient forms of Yoga founded by the Nath Tradition, such as Mahavatar Babaji Kriya Yoga. He bestows powerful Shaktipat transmissions and unique 'Thought Free' Sates of Raja Yoga which empower the practitioners to gradually go into Samadhi (awareness of one's own Self), experiencing the depths of Eternal Being. Lord Krishna's vision has given him to realize the oneness of all yogas, faiths and religions.

His Genius

Besides the Himalayan Masters, SatGurunath is the only Siddha known to us and broadly accessible, who gives authentic experiences of Shaktipat Kundalini Energy Transmission created specifically for spiritual and healing transformation essential to the awakening and continued evolution of humankind. The sincere will receive these dimensions of the Guru's consciousness through direct experience as to what true yoga is rather than through intellectual exploration. The experience of SatGurunath's Consciousness will be bestowed as the Guru guides the seeker in transforming his thought-filled finite mind into infinite consciousness free of thoughts.

Herein lies the Genius of Gurunath - with a flash he bestows upon you His Consciousness of Natural Enlightenment, transforming the ripples of thought in your mind's lake into a waveless lake of Soul Awareness bereft of thought. With flawless clarity during this passage he keeps intact the awareness of ones individual self as the boundaries of it's I-ness melt into the knowing of one's own boundless Awareness. This process he calls "Shivapat".

The mind's I-ness will resist its soul consciousness expanding into super consciousness out of fear of losing its ego identity. But this is not the truth. The complete truth is that the individual mind loses its identity only to partake its vaster identity as infinite awareness, the drop merges into the ocean not to lose itself but to become of it.

Panapat is the Uniqueness of Gurunath where with utter simplicity by breathing through us he brings to you Shiv Goraksha Babaji's Kriya Yoga and the Timeless Yoga of the Nath Yogis. He has simplified the arduous Nath techniques, yet preserved the effectiveness of the sacred practices. As a living master, he offers to humanity his own clear-mind consciousness. In sharing this experience with each individual seeker personally and with thousands of receptive people the world over simultaneously, Sat Gurunath as "The Presence" reveals the secret that at the level of pure consciousness all Humanity is One.

The Nath Lineage of Kriya Yoga

As we peer into the akashic records of the misty past we get a glimpse of the lineage of the Nath Yogis. It began from Adi Nath, Lord Shiva Himself, who gave it to His consort Parvati, Uday Nath. She gave it to Vishnu - Santosh Nath, Ganesh and Nandi Nath. Then Lord Krishna as Vishnu initiated Lord Vivasvat, the Spirit of our

Sun. The lineage was later guarded by the Kings of the Solar Dynasty: Vaivasvat Manu, King Ikshavaku down to Harishchandra, then to Lord Raghu Nath (Rama), 47th in descent from Ikshavaku. He is the 8th Rudra, esoterically connected with Shiv Goraksha Babaji, who is an incarnation of Lord Shiva Himself. It is through this grand lineage of the Nath Yogis that the royal science of Kriya Yoga has been preserved and handed down through the corridors of time by the ever-living Shiva- Goraksha-Babaji. It is to this lineage that Yogiraj Gurunath belongs – blessed by Babaji to spread this divine science in the East and West.

His Hallmark : The Knowing of a True Master

A Satguru or Empowering Master can be known by three distinct graces he bestows upon his disciples:

•Transmit – center to center in their pranic chakras – the evolutionary Kundalini Energy: Shaktipat
•Breathe the powerful breath through the breathing of disciples in their Spinal channels: Pranapat
•Impart his consciousness of thought free enlightenment to the receptive: Shivapat

Only a Master who showers all three blessings on truth seekers is a true Satguru. Gurunath bestows all three blessings.

Wings to Freedom – The Journey of the Soul

The way of the white swan is the evolution of human consciousness, the most comprehensive enterprise ever undertaken by humanity, besides which the greatest of human achievements pale into insignificance. This process is Yoga, which commends itself to the foremost minds of East and West. In the human brain exists the lateral ventricles in the shape of a "Swan in Flight" with its head pointing to the back as though the swan is flying faster than light back to the future. When the Hamsa Yogi, through meditation and pranayam, activates the Kundalini energy, then these ventricles in the brain open up. The two petals in the Agya Chakra, corresponding to the pituitary gland, open. The Yogi, at this stage, experiences Hamsa Consciousness, being breathed by the Divine Indweller.

The Sushumna channel in the spinal chord is the highway through which the Kundalini Energy travels and the evolution of consciousness takes place. It is the kinetic energy remaining after the completion of the universe. This force lies as light/sound vibrations potentially coiled around the swayambhu linga in the mooladhar chakra. To avail of it for one's own evolution and realization is the birthright of every human soul. It may be awakened by yogic procedures - best by Unmani, a no-mind state of absorption.

As the Hamsa Nath Yogi progresses in the Hamsa meditation, the third eye opens up in the Agya Chakra and he goes into the Sarvikalpa consciousness. Then, by further practice, he penetrates the Star of the Eye and expands to the Paramahamsa Nath Yogi state of Nirvikalpa consciousness, dwelling in the Cave of Brahma , the brain's third ventricle. Then his awareness evolves further beyond the I-ness of humanity to settle in the lateral swan-like ventricles of the brain, where he becomes the Siddha Nath Yogi. The mighty Hamsa soul has won its wings to freedom. As the subtle fibers of the Corona Radiata light up with Divine effulgence he takes flight into Cosmic consciousness as the Avadhoot Nath Yogi. He experiences the total Divinity of and beyond creation, gaining the ultimate knowledge of "Tat Tvam Asi" - "That Thou Art". The Yogi then merges into Niranjan, the final Nirvana, having attained the enlightenment of Buddha and Christ. This Avadhoot Nath Yogi returns to the world no more. If, under rare circumstances, he ever does, it will be the descent of Divinity as Avatar Nath Yogi.

SatGurunath's Vision for World Peace

Hear Our Soul Call!
If World Peace is to Herald the Dawn of a New Age,
realize that
Humanity Our Uniting Religion
Breath Our Uniting Prayer and
Consciousness Our Uniting God

www.ingramcontent.com/pod-product-compliance
Lightning Source LLC
Chambersburg PA
CBHW040407110426
42812CB00011B/2480